# CLINTONISMS:

## THE AMUSING, CONFUSING, AND SUSPECT MUSING OF BILLARY

*EDITED BY*
**JULIA GORIN**

CAMBRIDGE HOUSE PRESS
NEW YORK § TORONTO

Published by Cambridge House Press
New York, NY 10001
www.CamHousePress.com
For bulk purchases please contact specialsales@camhousepress.com

Library of Congress Cataloging-in-Publication Data

Clintonisms : the amusing, confusing, and suspect musing of Billary / edited by Julia Gorin.
    p. cm.
 ISBN 978-0-9787213-3-6
 1. Clinton, Bill, 1946--Quotations. 2. Clinton, Hillary Rodham--Quotations. 3. United States--Politics and government--1993-2001--Quotations, maxims, etc. 4. Arkansas--Politics and government--1951--Quotations, maxims, etc. 5. Clinton, Bill, 1946--Humor. 6. Clinton, Hillary Rodham--Humor. I. Gorin, Julia. II. Title.

 E886.2.C58 2007
 973.929092'2--dc22

                                        2007047001

Permission for all images given by Shutterstock, Inc. Cover design by Nicola Lengua. Clintonisms ™ Cambridge House Press.

10 9 8 7 6 5 4 3 2 1

Printed in the United States of America.

www.clintonisms.com

# ☆ Contents ☆

# ☆ Introduction ☆

Bill Clinton's post-presidential likeability is at an all-time high. With all forgiven, and a well-polled nostalgia for the Clinton era as well as the notion that getting Hillary means getting Bill back, we are faced with the very real possibility of another Clinton presidency. Which means the American public is setting itself up for a four- or eight-year reminder of what it is we've been forgiving the Clintons for. This book attempts to preempt that reminder and at the same time examine the pressing issues and questions that may be revisited in the event of a second Clinton presidency, questions as serious as a Clinton presidency itself.

For example, the question looms: If Bill Clinton was the first black president, would that make Hillary Clinton the second black president? Or is Bill Clinton a self-loathing brother who married a white woman and is a traitor to his race? Next, if there is any truth to the lesbian rumors about Hillary, will we compel our first female president to tell us who the real first lady is? Is there a JFK biography that Bill Clinton hasn't read? Why do the Clintons insist on getting pedigree dogs when all their dogs look the same in the end? Flat. Will Socks the Cat be re-adopted and resume his position as first prop? What about National Security Adviser Socks Berger?

Since re-electing the Clintons would mean that we officially sanction a sex addict as president, journalists could finally ask the questions they may have shied away from when we were only just acquainting ourselves with this new brand of presidency. Such as: Mr. Clinton, you have such a wonderful relationship with your daughter. What was it like going through puberty together? Have you managed to sustain your self-professed obsession with bin Laden even after finding out that Osama isn't a girl? Sir, if you found out you had only three hours left to live, would you have sex with Miss America again, or would you try to be faithful to your wife? (There is no right answer.)

During the first Clinton co-presidency, many comedians joked that the president's sex life is great—and the economy is great. Which means that if the Clintons win the erection, the economy could bounce back too. Further, with two complex, introspective, self-reflective leaders again in power, intellectually curious and concerned with looking inside themselves, there will be less focus on the outside, where enemies dwell and threaten to put a damper on our day. So the 1990s peace and prosperity could again ensue, proving that if we ignore our enemies they'll go away. This, in turn, could be the test to determine once and for all: Does Bill Clinton feel our pain, or does he cause it? Certainly the public felt his stain.

With a country that prefers a Social Worker-in-Chief to a Commander-in-Chief, we could shift our focus to things that truly threaten our way of life: third world poverty, climate change, hunger and obesity. AIDS would reclaim its Clintonian place as the nation's top security threat. On that subject, perhaps Bill Clinton might finally release his medical records, and tell us which brand of condoms his national security adviser recommended.

And still, there are more questions that need answering—indeed questions that a Clinton victory itself would answer. For example, is the public agreed that wiretapping is OK as long as one's political enemies, and not terrorists, are the targets? Is the Clinton Library considered American soil, or Chinese? Does a visitor need a passport to enter? How far will the enigmatic Clinton-Bush friendship go, and is Bob Dole jealous? What role, if any, has Viagra played in such developments?

As a steady supply of new and ever nervier scandals surfaces in response to public demand for the Clintons, will the apologists add to their repertoire of dismissals: We didn't elect them to be our moral compass. Don't these things go on in every administration? As long as he/she does his/her job...Isn't it time to move on? But he's apologized for his next three mistakes. Why do you hate them so? He's a flawed man...he's a flaw that looks like a man...There are all kinds of marriages...

Given the myriad TV documentaries out there on

the presidencies of Ronald Reagan, Lyndon Johnson and Richard Nixon, can we expect to see at least one on the Clinton presidency, perhaps titled "All the President's 'Hos"? (Once the networks figure out how to handle the NC-17 rating.)

After the successful Clinton-initiated repeal of the 22nd Amendment, which guarantees presidential term limits, we'll be able to do it all again, and again. Until one fine, distant, inconceivable day, the Clintons—by then well into their nineties—have exhausted all their possible presidencies. At that point, will we finally get to witness the Clinton divorce the couple have craved for so long? Will it be as amicable as the marriage? If so, will tickets be available?

This book is not a scholarly work and is not meant to be fair or balanced. It's a collection of anecdotes, reportage, jokes, and first, second and third-party quotes from and about the Clintons. The headers and taglines are original, and the quotes have been gleaned from the public domain: books, television, court testimony, interviews and press conferences. This work is meant, more than anything else, to convey the essence of that elusive creature, Billary.

JULIA GORIN

# Defining the Clintons

☆　☆　☆　☆　☆

**ISN'T THAT CALLED "DICTATORSHIP"?**
"Bill and I didn't come to Washington to do business as usual and compromise."

– Hillary Clinton, 1993

**TELL THAT TO MOTHER TERESA**
"The only way to make a difference is to acquire power."

– Hillary Clinton, during her senior year of college

**OH WELL**
"Politics gives guys so much power that they tend to behave badly around women. And I hope I never get into that."

– Bill Clinton, as a Rhodes scholar at Oxford, to a female acquaintance

### JUST LIKE BILL

"Too many people seem to think life is the tablecloth, instead of the messy feast that's spread out on it… That's not life. Done right, life leaves stains."

– Virginia Clinton, Bill Clinton's mother

### WELL, DID SHE GET THE COFFEE?

"She had gone on what she thought would be a great jog. She was going down to Battery Park, she was going to go around the towers. She was going to get a cup of coffee and—that's when the plane hit."

– Hillary Clinton, about daughter Chelsea, who watched the 9/11 attacks on TV about 40 blocks north of Ground Zero

### YOU MEAN KIND OF LIKE TOM CRUISE?

"It doesn't look good politically for me and Hillary not to have children, especially given the way Hillary is, and what people think about her."

– Bill Clinton, to Dolly Kyle Browning, a friend of Bill's, 1979

### I'LL JUST TAKE YOURS

"G--damn it, Bill. You promised me that office."

– Hillary Clinton, Inauguration Day, regarding the vice president's quarters, 1993

## COO COO CA-CHOO

"I'm not going to have some reporters pawing through our papers. We are the president."

– Hillary Clinton

## BUSH HAS ALL THE LUCK

"Former President Bill Clinton is described by friends as a frustrated spectator, unable to guide the nation through a crisis that is far bigger than anything he confronted in his eight-year tenure… A close friend of Mr. Clinton put it this way: 'He has said there has to be a defining moment in a presidency that really makes a great presidency. He didn't have one.'"

– Richard Berke, *The New York Times*, October 1, 2001

## HRC VOCAL TRAINING: me-me-me-me

"Oh, I am well aware that it is out there. One of the most difficult experiences that I personally had in the White House was during the health-care debate, being the object of extraordinary rage. I remember being in Seattle. I was there to make a speech about health care. This was probably August of '94. Radio talk-show hosts had urged their listeners to come out and yell and scream and carry on and prevent people from hearing me speak. There were threats that were coming in, and certain people didn't want me to speak, and they started taking weapons off people, and arresting people. I've had firsthand looks at this unreasoning anger and hatred that is focused on an individual you don't know, a cause that you despised—whatever motivates people."

– Hillary Clinton, response to a reporter's question about how she thought the American people would react to World Trade Center and Pentagon attacks now that they were on "the receiving end of a murderous anger," 2001

## IT WAS EITHER THAT OR "BUTCH"

"So when I was born, she called me Hillary, and she always told me it's because of Sir Edmund Hillary."

– Hillary Clinton, claiming that her mother named her after the climber six years *before* he became famous for climbing Mt. Everest, 1995

## HIS VIVID AND PAINFUL IMAGINATION

"I have vivid and painful memories of black churches being burned in my own state when I was a child."

– Bill Clinton, about his childhood in Arkansas, where there weren't any church burnings in that time period, June 8, 1996

## DID YOU HEAR THE ONE ABOUT THE IOWA CAUCUSES?

"Since I was a little boy, I've heard about the Iowa caucuses. That's why I would really like to do well in them."

– Bill Clinton, on the Iowa caucuses, which began in 1972 while Clinton was attending Oxford, February 12, 1996

## SO THAT'S WHAT KEEPS BILLARY GOING

"It's very hard to stop people who have no shame about what they're doing…who have never been acquainted with the truth."

– Hillary Clinton, ironically referring to Republican leadership, "Women for Hillary" breakfast, New York, June 6, 2005

## WHAT *IS* YOU TALKING ABOUT?

"It depends on what the meaning of the word 'is' is. If the—if he—if 'is' means is and never has been, that is not—that is one thing. If it means there is none, that was a completely true statement."

– Bill Clinton, August 17, 1998

## THAT EXPLAINS IT

"Clinton means what he says when he says it, but tomorrow he will mean what he says when he says the opposite. He is the existential president, living with absolute sincerity in the passing moment."

– Michael Kelly, *The New York Times Magazine*, July 31, 1994

"He's what [they call] the kind of a leader that finds out which way the crowd's going and then runs around and gets in front and says, 'follow me.'"

– *Arkansas Democrat-Gazette*

# 2

# The Clinton
# Presidential Race

☆　☆　☆　☆　☆

## BESIDES YOUR MOUTH?
"I want to run something."

– Hillary Clinton

## AND THEN THERE'LL BE NO REASON TO KEEP YOU AROUND
"Better make up your mind, Bill. If you don't run, I will."

– Hillary Clinton, 1992

## O SELFLESS ONE
"Not that I can imagine. No, that is not anything I have ever thought of for myself."

– Hillary Clinton, on running for president

## BLUE PLATE, BLUE DRESS—WHATEVER

"If you vote for my husband, you get me. It's a two-for-one blue plate special."

– Hillary Clinton, 1992

## AND A CIGAR AFICIONADO

"He's going to be president of the United States."

– Hillary Clinton

## 'HO-KEY DOKEY

"I want you to do damage control over Bill's philandering. I want you to get rid of all these b----es he's seeing… I want you to give me the names and addresses and phone numbers, and we can get them under control."

– Hillary Clinton, to private eye Ivan Duda, 1982

"Bill Clinton had a busy day on the campaign trail. He was in five states, seven cities and three flight attendants."

– David Letterman, comedian

# In Office

☆　☆　☆　☆　☆

### THE SUPPORTIVE FIRST LADY
"If I didn't kick Bill Clinton's a-- every day, he wouldn't be worth anything."

– Hillary Clinton

### HAPPY F---ING FLAG DAY
"Where is the G--damn f---ing flag? I want the G--damn f---ing flag up every f---ing morning at f---ing sunrise."

– Hillary Clinton, to her staff at the Governor's Mansion, Labor Day, 1991

### ...CAN BE LIKE CUBA?
"I pledge allegiance to the America that can be."

– Hillary Clinton, as recalled by Chris Matthews, "Hardball," November 2001

## VIVA LA REVOLUCIÓN
"We just can't trust the American people to make those types of choices. Government has to make those choices for people."

– Hillary Clinton, to Illinois Rep. Dennis Hastert about health care, 1993

## AND SOME DO IT AT THE SAME TIME—RIGHT, BRITNEY?
"You know, it's amazing to me that people actually stop at stop signs, that they do feed their children."

– Hillary Clinton, demonstrating her faith in humanity

## AND THE TAXES, OHH THOSE TAXES!
"I am a fan of the social policies that you find in Europe."

– Hillary Clinton, March 1996

## CONSTITUTION, SHMONSTITUTION

"We can't be so fixated on our desire to preserve the rights of ordinary Americans to legitimately own handguns and rifles."

– Bill Clinton, March 1993

"The purpose of the government is to rein in the rights of the people."

– Bill Clinton, on MTV, 1993

## GOVERNMENT OF THE GOVERNMENT BY THE GOVERNMENT FOR THE GOVERN-MENT

"If the personal freedoms guaranteed by the Constitution inhibit the government's ability to govern the people, we should look to limit those guarantees."

– Bill Clinton, August 12, 1993

## FEEL THE BURN

"[R]emaking of the American way of politics, government, indeed life… I have a burning desire to do what I can."

– Hillary Clinton

## AFTER ALL, A FUTURE COMMANDER-IN-CHIEF CAN'T RISK MILITARY SERVICE!

"First, I want to thank you, not just for saving me from the draft…"

– Bill Clinton, letter to the director of the University of Arkansas ROTC program, December 3, 1969

## DON'T TELL, DON'T TELL

"By every count, [Bill] was very neglectful of the military. I don't think he understood it. I don't think he liked it. And it was a very bad period for the military. Morale was very low."

– Casper Weinberger, former Secretary of Defense for Ronald Reagan, November 29, 2001

## SUBCONSCIENTIOUS OBJECTOR

"Because of my opposition to the draft and the war, I am in great sympathy with those who are not willing to fight, kill, and maybe die for their country… I am writing too in the hope that my telling this one story will help you to understand more clearly how so many fine people have come to find themselves still loving their country but loathing the military."

– Bill Clinton, letter to the director of the University of Arkansas ROTC program, December 3, 1969

## HAMBURGER HILL

**Hillary:** I decided that I was very interested in having some experience in serving in some capacity in the military.

**Bill:** Because we all love the military so much.

**Hillary:** So I walked into our local [Marine] recruiting office... This young man looked at me and he said, "How old are you?"...I said, "Well, twenty-seven,"...I had these really thick glasses on. He said, "How bad's your eyesight?" I said, "It's pretty bad." And he finally said to me, "You're too old. You can't see. And you're a woman." He said, "But maybe the dogs [Army] would take you." This [was] not a very encouraging conversation... So [I thought] maybe I'll look for another way to serve my country.

– Hillary and Bill Clinton, concerning Hillary's stated 1975 attempt to join the military, television interview, 1994

## ROOTING FOR A TIE

"The many fans here wanted the American team to win. They were all so great, if I were not a partisan, you almost hate to see either side lose."

– Bill Clinton, lamenting that the American team beat the Chinese team at the Women's World Cup Soccer finals in Pasadena, CA, July 1999

# 4

# A Note of Thanks for All You Do

☆　☆　☆　☆　☆

**BESIDES, PICKLE JARS CAN BE TRICKY**
"[We] have nothing but praise for their courage, integrity, and professionalism, and we feel lucky to remain friends with many agents who protected us."

– Hillary Clinton

**DECENCY IS IN THE DETAILS**
"If you want to remain on this detail, get your f---ing a-- over here and grab those bags!"

– Hillary Clinton, to a Secret Service agent for whom toting bags is against regulation

## SILENT PARTNER

"F--- off! It's enough that I have to see you s---kickers every day. I'm not going to talk to you, too. Just do your G--damn job and keep your mouth shut."

– Hillary Clinton, to an Arkansas State Trooper bodyguard in response to "Good morning, Mrs. Clinton"

## P.S.

"[You] f---ing idiot."

– Hillary Clinton, to her driver in Arkansas

## NOT TO MENTION THEIR PANTS

"Have you ever seen anyone losing their temper? And how people lose control of their good sense in moments of passion?"

– Hillary Clinton

## B---- ON WINGS

"Put this on the ground! I left my sunglasses in the limo. I need those sunglasses. We need to go back!"

– Hillary Clinton, after her airplane takeoff

## PARDON ME
"Get f---ed!"

– Hillary Clinton, shoving a Secret Service agent out of her way

## AS YOU WISH, M' LORD
"Get the f--- out of my way!"

– Hillary Clinton, as reported in a complaint filed by a Secret Service officer in early 2000

## STORM TROOPER
"We all got used to her screaming, 'Just get the hell away from me.'"

– Arkansas State Trooper, whom Hillary tried to kick

## LEFT-WINGED LITERACY
"Ouch."

– Secret Service agent, after Hillary Clinton threw a book at the back of his head, according to White House military personnel

## THE S---KICKERS/IDIOTS ARE CATCHING ON
"Get off the stage! We don't want you here!"

– New York City police officer, to Hillary Clinton at "Concert for New York," amid jeering and booing from thousands of firemen and police at Madison Square Garden, October 2001

## MEETING MISTERS RIGHT

"She was really upset by the response because of how unexpected it was, there was no way of seeing it coming."

– Top Clinton source, October 21, 2001

## SHE DIDN'T?

"How could we not know this would be the wrong forum for Hillary?! These are cops and firemen who listen to right-wing talk radio. They still think she killed Vince Foster, for Christ's sake!"

– Clinton confidante

## SINCE OTHERWISE THERE'S NOTHING EM-BARRASSING ABOUT US

"[The Secret Service] will shut down the entire Eastern Seaboard just to embarrass us if we give them the excuse… They do this to us all the time. They're mainly Republicans. They hate us. They always take the most extreme option just to cause us embarrassment."

– Hillary Clinton

# 5

# Laws? Those are for Opponents!

☆　☆　☆　☆　☆

## NO WONDER SHE WANTS NEW LAWS, SHE CAN'T SEEM TO FOLLOW THE OLD ONES

"I really believe in campaign finance reform...we have to change this system."

– Hillary Clinton, March 2000

"In the filings that Hillary's campaign filed with the FEC, they had entirely omitted any reference to my [$1.2 million] contributions."

– 2007 Campaign donor and fundraiser

## IT'S A FAMILY TRADITION

"Larry, I am the governor of the state of Arkansas. I work really hard and the laws that apply to everyone else shouldn't apply to me."

– Bill Clinton, to State Trooper Larry Patterson, Clinton's bodyguard from 1986-92

## MYSELF BEING THE EXCEPTION

"Research shows the presence of women raises the standards of ethical behavior and lowers corruption."

– Hillary Clinton, on women in government being less corrupt than men, New York, March 2005

## AND HE DOESN'T MEAN CONNECTICUT

"Now what we're talking about here is the largest election law fraud in the history of the United States… Hillary's skill has been in seeing to it that obvious crimes didn't reach the level of being placed in front of a jury. Because if they ever had, she might have been baking cookies from the same place that Martha Stewart did."

– Constitutional Law Specialist, from the documentary *Hillary Uncensored*

## IF ONLY

"I suppose I could've stayed home and baked cookies and had teas…"

– Hillary Clinton, response to Jerry Brown's criticisms about her questionable business transactions in the 1980s, 1992

### I TAKE MY TEA BOTH WAYS, THANK YOU
"I've made my share of cookies and served hundreds of cups of tea...so it never occurred to me that my comment would be taken as insulting to mothers."

– Hillary Clinton

### DO YOU NEED A REARVIEW MIRROR FOR THAT BACKPEDALING?
"Besides, I've done quite a lot of cookie-baking in my day, and tea-pouring, too."

– Hillary Clinton, in her book, *Living History*

### HE HAS ALWAYS BEEN HANDSY IN THE KITCHEN
"I wouldn't put anything past Bill Clinton."

– Kathy Fergusen, whom Bill allegedly once pinned against the kitchen counter in the Governor's Mansion

## SO IT'S BEEN GOOD FOR YOU BOTH?

"Since I don't have access to the White House pastry chef anymore, it's done wonders for my figure."

– Bill Clinton, July 2001

## IF THERE'S NOT ENOUGH HEAT, GET IN THE KITCHEN

"A White House pastry chef has sued President Clinton and her former boss, the charge being that the head pastry chef Roland Mesnier retaliated when she rebuffed his sexual advances and that the White House failed to respond to the complaints... She charges that Clinton, as head of the White House, failed to carry out his duty under the 1996 Presidential and Executive Office Accountability Act (PEOAA), which directed the president to establish rules extending civil rights protection to all employees by October 1997."

– *The Washington Post*, September 2000

## PLEASE, NO ONE OVER 25

"Bill Clinton's office, located at 55 West 125th Street, is seeking interns in its understaffed scheduling department."

– Help wanted email, to the political science department at Columbia University, November 2001

## NO—STAY OUT OF THE KITCHEN!

"In general, if he needed assistance and his assistant was busy I would be asked to do anything basic. The guy said Mr. Clinton might need help in his kitchen, and I would do that."

– Columbia University student, who interviewed for the position but turned it down, as profiled in *The New Yorker*

# 6

# Games First-Couples Play

☆　☆　☆　☆　☆

## WHERE THERE IS (CIGAR) SMOKE...

**Q:** If Monica Lewinsky says that you used a cigar as a sexual aid with her in the Oval Office area, would she be lying? Yes, no, or won't answer?

**A:** I will revert to my former statement.

– Bill Clinton, grand jury testimony, August 17, 1998

## ...THERE IS FIRE

"You'd better put some ice on that."

– Bill Clinton, to Juanita Broaddrick in reference to her swollen lip that he bit while allegedly raping her in 1978, *The Wall Street Journal*, February 19, 1999

## SOMETHING EVERY LITTLE GIRL NEEDS

"The fact of the matter is, I've always been a Yankees fan. I am a Cubs fan, but I needed an American League team…so as a young girl, I became very interested and enamored of the Yankees."

– Hillary Clinton

## BUT HE SURE MAKES IT LOOK LIKE ONE

"This is not a sport, this is a solemn responsibility. [Young people should not have sex] when they're not prepared to marry the others, they're not prepared to take responsibility for the children and they're not even able to take responsibility for themselves."

– Bill Clinton, to a group of Southeast Washington high school students, March 1994

## WHO SAYS BILL CLINTON WASN'T A ROLE MODEL?

"The kids' definitions were different. They were a bit closer to President Clinton's definition. They said petting or touching wasn't sex. Oral sex wasn't sex…[A] government report that says the percentage of high school kids having sex dropped this past decade to 46 percent…[said] more are having oral sex."

– "20/20," December 6, 2002

## LET'S FINISH WITH A GAME OF ECHO

"There is nothing wrong with America that cannot be cured by what is right with America."

– Bill Clinton, Inauguration Speech, January 20, 1993

"There is nothing wrong with America that cannot be fixed by what is right about America."

– Hillary Clinton, premature Inauguration Speech, April 2007

# 7

# Whitewater and Post-Pardon Depression

☆　☆　☆　☆　☆

**IL(GOTTEN)LOGIC**

"If we did something improper, then how come we lost money?"

– Hillary Clinton

**PLUS, NOBODY IMPORTANT LIVES IN A TRAILER PARK**

"Castle Grande was a trailer park on a piece of property that was about a thousand acres big. I never did any work on Castle Grande."

– Hillary Clinton, on "20/20," January 1996

## DOTH THE LADY PROTEST TOO MUCH?

"Oh, that didn't happen, and I know nothing about any other such stories."

– Hillary Clinton, to a reporter asking what she knew about stories of shredding Whitewater documents in Arkansas, April 1994

"The billing records show I did not do work for Castle Grande. I did work for something called IDC, which was not related to Castle Grande."

– Hillary Clinton, on "20/20," January 1996

"It was always the same thing. As far as I know, IDC and Castle Grande were one and the same."

– Former Clinton business partner Susan McDougal, on "Nightline," January 30, 1996

## DEPENDING ON WHAT THE MEANING OF "IT" IS

"It appears I cooperated with this effort—to dispose of such files."

– Hillary Clinton, sworn statement to the Resolution Trust Corporation, January 15, 1996

## ANOTHER FUTURE EX-PRESIDENT WITH ALZHEIMER'S?

"It is possible that I did once know something more that would be responsive to these interrogatories, but if I did, I do not recall it now."

– Hillary Clinton, sworn statement

## WHAT'S SIX MONTHS OF MISSING FILES COMPARED TO 18 MINUTES OF MISSING TAPE?

"The problem back then, you'll remember, is that documents were destroyed, tapes were missing 18 and a half minutes. The White House was not cooperating… I think the contrast is so dramatic."

– Hillary Clinton, on Richard Nixon

## TO THE TRAVEL OFFICE STAFF: TAKE OFF

"We need those people out. We need our people in."

– Hillary Clinton, in released memos from several White House aides

"But I did not make the decisions, I did not direct anyone to make the decisions. But I have absolutely no doubt that I did express concern, because I was concerned about any kind of financial mismanagement."

– Hillary Clinton, regarding the travel office firings

## I DIDN'T EVEN KNOW I HAD A BROTHER

"I knew nothing about my brother's involvement in these pardons. I knew nothing about his taking money for his involvement… I had no knowledge whatsoever."

– Hillary Clinton, press conference, February 2001

## BUCK PASSER

"[I] never knew about Marc Rich at all. You know, people would hand me envelopes; I would just pass them… I knew nothing about the Marc Rich pardon until after it happened."

– Hillary Clinton, February 2001

"In a new poll, 47 percent of New Yorkers said they would like former President Clinton to run for mayor of New York. Apparently, this is the same 47 percent of New Yorkers that were pardoned by him."

– Conan O'Brien, comedian

# 8

# Billary's Opinion on Impeachment

☆　☆　☆　☆　☆

## NOT TO MENTION THEIR CAMPAIGN AGAINST BLUE M&Ms

"The case for impeachment was part of a political war waged by people determined to sabotage the president's agenda on the economy, education, Social Security, health care, the environment and the search for peace in Northern Ireland, the Balkans, and the Middle East."

– Hillary Clinton

## WOMAN IN COMBAT

"Bill had been blindsided, and the unfairness of it all made me more determined to stand with him to combat the charges."

– Hillary Clinton

## BILL'S CASE FOR DEFUNDING THE FBI AND CIA

"I think the country could be spared a lot of agony and the government could worry about inflation and a lot of other problems if [Nixon would] go on and resign. [There is] no question that an admission of making false statements to government officials and interfering with the FBI and the CIA is an impeachable offense."

– Bill Clinton, during the Nixon investigations, August 1974

## WE THOUGHT IT WAS A VAST RIGHT-WING CONSPIRACY ATTACKING HER HUSBAND, BUT IT'S...

"Keep that b---- away from me! I don't want to do anything that'll get me in more trouble."

– Bill Clinton, to a Secret Service agent, after Hillary clocked him "upside the head" and threw a lamp at him the day that the Articles of Impeachment were passed against him (not on the day she found out about the affair), December 1998

**9**

# Behind Every Lying Man
# Lies a Woman

☆ ☆ ☆ ☆ ☆

**APPARENTLY STILL A VIRGIN**

"I am going to say this again: I did not have sexual relations with that woman, Miss Lewinsky."

– Bill Clinton, January 26, 1998

**SO HELP YOU GOD?**

"What the president has told the nation is the whole truth and nothing but."

– Hillary Clinton

**Q:** Did you have an extramarital sexual affair with Monica Lewinsky?
**A:** No.

– Bill Clinton, grand jury testimony, August 17, 1998

## OR ON ME

"My husband may have his faults, but he has never lied to me."

– Hillary Clinton

## HE HOLDS THESE TRUTHS TO BE SELF-EVIDENT

**Q:** The grand jury would like to know, Mr. President, why it is that you think that oral sex performed on you does not fall within the definition of sexual relations as used in this deposition.

**A:** Because that is if the deponent is the person who has oral sex performed on him, then the contact is with not with anything on that list, but with the lips of another person. It seems to be self-evident that that's what it is. And I thought it was curious.

– Bill Clinton, grand jury testimony, August 17, 1998

## *THEY* TOUCHED *ME*!

**Q:** If Monica Lewinsky says that while you were in the Oval Office area you touched her breasts, would she be lying?

**A:** That is not my recollection. My recollection is that I did not have sexual relations with Ms. Lewinsky. And I'm staying on my former statement about that.

– Bill Clinton, grand jury testimony, August 17, 1998

## LIAR OR PHILOSOPHER?

**Q:** Do you agree with me that the statement, "I was never alone with her," is incorrect? You were alone with Monica Lewinsky, weren't you?

**A:** Well again…it depends on how you define alone.

– Bill Clinton, grand jury testimony, August 17, 1998

## OR THAT SHE OWNS A DRESS

"Just because his semen is on her dress doesn't mean they had sex."

– Democratic operative, 1998

## IT TAKES ONE TO KNOW ONE

"She is such a liar… She's crazy, unstable, and totally dishonest. You can't trust a thing she says."

– Hillary Clinton, to Clinton adviser Dick Morris, about Susan McDougal—before it was clear that the latter would be keeping quiet about Whitewater

## BESIDES, HIS SEX LIFE IS NONE OF MY BUSINESS

"He ministers to troubled people all the time… If you knew his mother you would understand."

– Hillary Clinton, to Sidney Blumenthal, about Bill's relationship with Monica Lewinsky

## EXCEPT THAT'S EXACTLY HIS TYPE

"Who's going to find out? These women are all trash. Nobody's going to believe them."

– Hillary Clinton, during 1992 campaign

## BESIDES BILL

"Drag a hundred-dollar bill through a trailer park, you never know what you'll find."

– Clinton adviser, about Paula Jones

## TRYING TO KEEP IT ALL STRAIGHT

"She came on to me, right?"

– Bill Clinton, to Betty Currie, reviewing the testimony she was about to give

## WILT CHAMBERLAIN HAS BEEN THROUGH 20,000

"I'm not sitting here like some little woman standing by my man like Tammy Wynette. I'm sitting here because I love him and I honor what he's been through and what we've been through together."

– Hillary Clinton, 1992

## I LIKE BOTH KINDS OF MUSIC

"I didn't mean to hurt Tammy Wynette…I happen to be a country-western fan."

– Hillary Clinton

## AND MY UNNATURAL ONES

"I'm just trying to suppress my natural impulses and get back to work."

– Bill Clinton, on "The News Hour with Jim Lehrer," January 1998

## 101 WAYS TO SAY YOU'RE SORRY (FOR GETTING CAUGHT)

"What I want the American people to know, what I want the Congress to know is that I am profoundly sorry for all I have done wrong in words and deeds. I never should have misled the country, the Congress, my friends or my family. Quite simply, I gave in to my shame."

– Bill Clinton, December 1998

## I'M SORRY THIS IS BEING DONE TO ME

"Mere words cannot fully express the profound remorse I feel for what our country is going through."

– Bill Clinton, December 1998

## IF HE DOES SAY SO HIMSELF

"I made a bad personal mistake. I paid a big price for it."

– Bill Clinton, June 1, 2005

"I made a terrible public, personal mistake, but I paid for it many times over."

– Bill Clinton, to Peter Jennings, November 18, 2004

## ESPECIALLY THE FRENCH

"I'm sorry for the American people, and I'm sorry for the embarrassment [that investigators] performed. But they ought to think about the way the rest of the world reacted to it… I got a standing ovation at the United Nations from the whole world…"

– Bill Clinton, to Peter Jennings, November 18, 2004

## TO THE NEXT GIRL

"Now it is time—in fact, it is past time to move on."

– Bill Clinton, in a speech to the American public, August 17, 1998

## IN THE END, AMBITION…ER…LOVE CONQUERS ALL

"Why can't anybody understand that I truly love this man?"

– Hillary Clinton

"Bill and I have always loved each other… I'm proud of my marriage."

– Hillary Clinton

"From my perspective, our marriage is a strong marriage. We love each other."

– Hillary Clinton

## A GOOD STRETCH OF HIM NOT GETTING CAUGHT

"You know, we did have a very good stretch…years and years of nothing—I thought this was resolved ten years ago."

– Hillary Clinton, on CBS "Evening News," August 1999

## THE RING THAT FREUDIAN SLIPPED

"He basically forgot…he has never seen Bill Clinton without his wedding band, and apologizes for the mistake."

– "Inside Edition," referring to painter Nelson Shanks, who omitted Clinton's wedding band from the Presidential portrait, April 26, 2006

## AND IF THERE'S ONE THING BILL LOVES MORE THAN BURGERS...

"'Up and down this street is where they all come. You get the shortest shorts and the shortest skirts here,' McLarty drooled. 'Burger King is also good.'"

– *New York Post*, on the Harlem location for Bill Clinton's offices, July 30, 2001

# 10

# The Black Panderers

☆ ☆ ☆ ☆ ☆

### OR DESTROY THE COUNTRY TRYING

"This reminds me of one of my favorite American heroines, Harriet Tubman. She kept going back down South to bring other freed slaves to freedom. And she used to say, 'No matter what happens, keep going.' So we're going to keep going until we take back the White House!"

– Hillary Clinton, Al Sharpton civil rights group fundraiser, April 2007

### WEEPING BILLO

"I was in my living room in Hot Springs, Arkansas. I remember the chair I was sitting in; I remember exactly where it was in the room; I remember exactly the position of the chair when I sat and watched on national television the great March on Washington unfold. I remember weeping uncontrollably during

Martin Luther King's speech, and I remember thinking when it was over, my country would never be the same and neither would I."

– Bill Clinton, speech commemorating the 35th anniversary of the March on Washington, August 28, 1998

### ACTUALLY WE DON'T

"When you look at the way the House of Representatives has been run, it has been run like a plantation, and you know what I'm talkin' about."

– Hillary Clinton, Martin Luther King Day celebration, Harlem, January 16, 2006

### AND THE ALLEY-OOP

"They looked beyond the color of my skin into the content of my heart...[Black Americans gave me] a lifetime of education in the importance of mutual respect, reconciliation and recognizing our common humanity."

– Bill Clinton, on his induction into Arkansas' Black Hall of Fame, October 2002

### TEENA MARIE, DEBBIE DEAN, KIKI DEE, AND THE MESSENGERS?

"Motown, Motown, that's my era. Those are my people."

– Hillary Clinton, on New York radio station Hot 97, during the 2000 senatorial race

### THE UNITER
"If it had been a young white man, in a young all-white neighborhood, it probably wouldn't have happened."

– Bill Clinton, about Amadou Diallo, fundraiser, California, March 3, 2000

### WHAT I MEAN IS...BLACK PEOPLE ARE EXTRAORDINARY!
"African-Americans watch the same news at night that ordinary Americans do."

– Bill Clinton, on B.E.T., November 2, 1994

### THE CUDDLY PANDER BEAR
"That's why I went to Harlem, because I think I am the first black president."

– Bill Clinton, 32nd NAACP Image Awards, where he received the President's Award, March 4, 2001

## HOW ABOUT A NICE PIED-Á-TERRE ON THE MOON?

"Harlem is a sharp contrast [to] the posh, predominantly white neighborhood in midtown Manhattan where Clinton had initially planned to rent office space."

– *The Morning Sun*, February 14, 2001

## GIVE A (S)EX-PRESIDENT SOME SPACE

"The ex-president was blasted by taxpayer watchdog groups earlier this year when he chose an 8,500-square-foot office on the 56th floor of Carnegie Hall Towers in midtown Manhattan that would have cost taxpayers $811,000 a year—more than the cost of the offices of all the other ex-presidents combined."

– Newsmax, April 19, 2001

## AN ACTUAL BLACK MAN HAD TO COME UP WITH THE IDEA

"Harlem Congressman Charles Rangel [called] Clinton over the weekend…to recommend the move to Clinton."

– Jonah Goldberg, JewishWorldReview.com, February 2001

## KEEPIN' IT UNREAL

"It feels like coming home."

– Bill Clinton, while strolling through Harlem, February 2001

## MCDONALD'S OPENED THREE NEW HARLEM LOCATIONS JUST IN CASE

"After all other suitable office space in Manhattan had dried up... Clinton announced he would take an office in Harlem... Even Al Sharpton doesn't expect Mr. Hollywood to be spending his days at the Harlem site."

– Ann Coulter, February 2001

## YOU BEEN SERVED

"'I want to make sure I'm a good neighbor in Harlem,' (Bill Clinton) said. In the past two years, however... people say they have occasionally seen him, under Secret Service guard, ducking through the back door of his office—if, that is, they have seen him at all."

– *The New York Times*, November 17, 2003

## BUT HE'S A GLOBETROTTER

"Many people come around to ask about you, sir. It has happened maybe 10 or 15 times. I have to tell them that you are not around."

– Coffee cart operator outside Clinton's office

## DISSSSSSSSSSSSSSS!

"I've heard of him. Seen him? No."

– McDonald's employee, at a location a few storefronts down from Clinton's office

## TAKE A NUMBER, TOOTS

"I love you, Bill, but I need to see you more."

– Department of Veterans Affairs worker, to Bill Clinton in the elevator, October 2003

## THE FIRST BLAXPLOITATION PRESIDENT

"He exploited black sentiment because he knew the rituals of black culture. Bill Clinton exploited us like no president before him."

– Michael Eric Dyson, professor of religious studies at DePaul University, Chicago, at a Detroit fundraiser for the NAACP

## HE BELONGS IN THE ARSENIO HALL OF FAME

"[W]e had been neglected by so many previous administrations that [we accepted] the first man who came by and winked at us and played saxophone on 'Arsenio Hall.'

Well, shame on so many African Americans for holding Bill Clinton up as some sort of hero."

– Charles Barron, New York City Council member, NAACP 47th annual fundraising dinner

## ALSO THE FIRST JEWISH PRESIDENT, APPARENTLY

"If Iraq came across the Jordan River… I would grab a rifle and get in the trench and fight and die [defending Israel]."

– Bill Clinton, Hadassah-Wizo Organization fundraiser, Toronto, July 30, 2002

## IS THAT A EUPHEMISM FOR SOMETHING?

"Clinton isn't headed into any ditches with any guns to defend Israel. If he can't plug in his blow-dryer, he ain't going."

– Monica Crowley, WABC Radio Host, August 2002

## ACTUALLY, THE FIRST BLACK-JEWISH-MUSLIM PRESIDENT

"[T]here was this appalling example in northern Europe, in Denmark…these totally outrageous cartoons against Islam."

– Bill Clinton, economic conference, Qatar, January 2006

## HEY, ME TOO!

"I am pleased that since last year the State Department has inaugurated a new website entitled 'Islam in America.' Its purpose is to help people everywhere learn more about the positive force that Islam has become in American life and about the growing role of Muslim Americans as they are there to play a role in ensuring the security, prosperity, and freedom of our land."

– Hillary Clinton, at the second White House Iftar meal, Ramadan 2000

## EXPLAINS A LOT

"I have to admit that a good deal of what my husband and I have learned [about Islam] has come from my daughter. [As] some of you who are our friends know, she took a course last year in Islamic history."

– Hillary Clinton, addressing members of the American Muslim Council, first U.S. presidential reception celebrating Eid al-Fitr, February 20, 1996

## NO, WAIT—HE WAS THE FIRST BLACK-JEWISH-MUSLIM-NATIVE-AMERICAN PRESIDENT

"My grandmother was one-quarter Cherokee."

– Bill Clinton, amid criticism from American Indians that his race initiative ignores them

## A STATE OF MIND

"If you lived in Arkansas...give it up."

– Cherokee Heritage Center genealogist, who said that the roots of the tribe are in Oklahoma, Texas, and North Carolina

## AND DON'T FORGET ABOUT THE HISPANICS

"[Clinton Elementary] represents the diversity and strength of America...[California] has no majority race or ethnic group... I guarantee you someday we will elect a Hispanic, woman president of the United States."

– Bill Clinton, William Jefferson Clinton Elementary School on East Compton Boulevard, Los Angeles, September 2003

## ALL THINGS TO ALL PEOPLE...INCLUDING RICH, BLACK ATHLETES

"You worked very hard...I think there ought to be new rules for athletes."

– Bill Clinton, congratulatory phone call to Venus Williams for winning the 2000 U.S. Open, during which she asked, "Can you lower my taxes, please?"

## HE'S A WOMAN TOO!

"Am I proud that I got a chance to appoint the first woman Secretary of State? You bet I am. My Mama is smiling down on me right now."

– Bill Clinton

## CABINET, HAREM, WHAT'S THE DIFFERENCE?

"I would not restrict myself to having just half the Cabinet be women. I might want more."

– Bill Clinton, February 29, 1992

# 11

# Sax, Drugs, & Rock 'n' Roll

☆　☆　☆　☆　☆

## JUST SAY ~~NO~~ "I DIDN'T INHALE" TO DRUGS

"I'm thinking of saying I never violated the drug laws of my country."

– Bill Clinton, response when asked how he was planning to handle the question of marijuana use, 1991

## USING MY DEFINITION OF "BROKEN"

"[I've never] broken any drug law."

– Bill Clinton, 1991

## IT SAYS HIGH

"No, I wouldn't know if I saw it."

– Bill Clinton, response to a reporter asking whether or not he'd used cocaine, 1986

## TAKING THE HIGH ROAD

I experimented with marijuana a time or two. And I didn't like it, and didn't inhale, and never tried it again.

– Bill Clinton, March 31, 1992

## A NOSE FOR POLITICS

"I've got to get some for my brother. He's got a nose like a Hoover vacuum cleaner."

– Roger Clinton, as recorded by an Arkansas police detective, 1984

## AND 40 YEARS LATER I *KNOW* THERE ARE NO CONSEQUENCES

"When I was twenty-two years old, in England, and I thought there were no consequences, I tried marijuana a couple of times."

– Bill Clinton, town hall discussion, 1997

## THAT YOU MORONS WOULD ACTUALLY PUT ME IN THE WHITE HOUSE, FOR INSTANCE

"But if I had known then what I know now, I would not have done it."

– Bill Clinton, same town hall discussion, 1997

## AND SOME TO ALL OF THE ABOVE

"I think we're all addicted to something. Some people are addicted to drugs. Some to power. Some to food. Some to sex. We're all addicted to something."

– Bill Clinton, mid 1980s, to friends about his brother Roger's cocaine addiction, *The Washington Post*, January 25, 1998

## HE'S A ROCK STAR AFTER ALL

### THE TSNUMANI TOUR!

"Rested Clinton goes back on tsunami tour."

– *Chicago Sun-Times*, May 30, 2005

### THE OBESITY TOUR!

"He's going to start by talking to kids, visiting schools around the country and telling his story. He was overweight as a child…"

– *TIME Magazine*, July 24, 2005

### THE AIDS TOUR!

"Former President Bill Clinton today pledged to become a traveling campaigner in the effort to rally increased governmental commitment and political leadership in the global effort to prevent AIDS and treat people affected by it."

– *The New York Times,* July 13, 2002

## THE CLIMATE CHANGE TOUR!

"And the new energy future is decentralized, entrepreneurial and needs people like you to say, 'Give me a clean car, give me solar shingles to put on my roof—give me a clean future.'"

– Bill Clinton, opening for The Rolling Stones at the Staples Center in Los Angeles, Febuary 2003

## THE FAREWELL TOUR!

"He's going around the country…basically thanking himself for being our president."

– Chris Matthews, on MSNBC, referring to the longest goodbye in presidential history, 2001

"Clinton made a stop in Chicago yesterday continuing his cross-country farewell tour as the president… The tour was an emotional one, as it may be the last time for thousands of young Americans to see their father."

– Craig Kilborn, comedian

## NOT "HOUND DOG"?

**Katie Couric**: The entertainer of the century?

**Clinton:** For me in my lifetime…the early Elvis would be the best.

**Katie Couric:** Your favorite Elvis song?

**Clinton:** "I Want You…I Need You…I Love You."

– "Today Show," December 20, 1999

## ALWAYS AN ORIGINAL

"Bill sort of identified with Elvis."

– Hillary Clinton

## BILLY THE KING

"A peanut butter and banana sandwich was one of his favorite things. I got him his own jar of peanut butter because he didn't necessarily use a knife to eat peanut butter directly out of the jar."

– Bill Clinton's roommate, on Clinton and Elvis Presley's favorite snack, mid 1970s

"Bill Clinton was busy over the weekend at a casino where he was playing saxophone. It's hard to believe, isn't it, that since this guy has left office he's actually become less classy."

– David Letterman, comedian

# 12

# The Clinton Philosophy of Marriage

☆ ☆ ☆ ☆ ☆

**SUCH AS WOMEN**

"We talk about everything, and have for as long as we've known each other…particularly on issues where we share a common commitment."

– Hillary Clinton

**TO WIN IT**

"The only two people who count in any marriage are the two who are in it."

– Hillary Clinton

**NO CHIDE LEFT BEHIND**

"Come back here, you a--hole! Where the f--- do you think you're going?"

– Hillary Clinton, to Bill

## OR PUT HER BACK IN THE CAKE

"What the f--- do you think you're doing? I know who that whore is. I know what she's here for. Get her out of here."

– Hillary Clinton, to Larry Patterson, for bringing a GFOB (girlfriend of Bill) to a ceremony, January 1993

## FAILING THAT, I'LL JUST TAKE THE PRESIDENCY

"I want to go to supper with my husband, I want to go the movies. I want to go on vacation with my family. I want my husband back."

– Hillary Clinton

## CLINTON LULLABY

"I want a div-or-or-or-orce. I want a div-or-or-or-orce."

– Bill Clinton, singing to one-year-old Chelsea on the living room floor, as overheard by a friend and related to a former *Washington Post* reporter

## I HANDLE ALL OF MY OWN INVESTMENTS

"I know the truth of my life and of my marriage, my relationship and partnership, my deep abiding friendship with my husband... I never doubted that it was a marriage worth investing in, even in the midst of those challenges, and I'm really happy that I made that decision."

– Hillary Clinton, 2007

## AFTER WE MAKE IT BETTER FOR OUR-SELVES

"[Bill] and I really are bound together in part because we believe we have an obligation to give something back and to be part of making life better for other people."

– Hillary Clinton

## FUNNY, THAT'S BILL'S FAVORITE QUESTION TOO

"Politics is how we get along with one another. How we compromise with each other. When someone says to me, 'How can you stand being involved in politics?' I always say, 'Are you married?'"

– Hillary Clinton

## THEY MUST HAVE NEEDED HELP WITH ALL THOSE SKELETONS

"We just stayed home and cleaned closets."

– Hillary Clinton

## I WONDER WHAT YOUR MARRIAGE SAYS ABOUT OUR FUTURE

"I wonder what history is going to say about our marriage."

– Hillary Clinton

"In Hillary Clinton's new book *Living History*, Hillary details what it was like meeting Bill Clinton, falling in love with him, getting married, and living a passionate, wonderful life as husband and wife.
Then on page two, the trouble starts."

– Jay Leno, comedian

# 13

# Being President is Hard, Not Being President is Harder

☆　☆　☆　☆　☆

**CLINSTRADAMUS**

"The office of the president is such that it calls for a higher level of conduct than expected from the average citizen of the United States."

– Hillary Clinton, calling for the impeachment of Nixon, 1974

**IN RELATED NEWS, 60% OF U.S. SPOTLIGHTS HAVE BEEN LAID OFF**

"Ex-President Bill Clinton may be seeing a psychiatrist in an effort to adjust to private life, a report out of Chicago suggests…[S]ince leaving the White House, Clinton is having a difficult time coping with life out of the spotlight."

– *Newsmax Magazine*, September 2002

## HY ON EARTH OULD THAT BE HYSTERICAL?

"Wouldn't it be hysterical if someone just happened to remove all the w's from the computer keyboards?"

– Hillary Clinton, January 19, 2001

## ONCE YOU POP, YOU JUST CAN'T STOP

"The General Accounting Office...report found that missing and damaged property included 62 keyboards, 26 cell phones, two cameras, 10 antique doorknobs, five to 10 presidential medallions, and a number of office signs... Last year, the GAO began an investigation and received photographic details from the White House, including pictures of obscene graffiti; a presidential seal ripped from a wall; 10 sliced telephone lines; dozens of phones and keyboards that had been tampered with; and thousands of office supplies dumped in the trash."

– FoxNews.com, June 2002

## JUST BRING THE SAX

"I have this recurring nightmare that for the first four or five months after I leave office, I'll be lost every time I enter a room because nobody will be playing a song. I won't know where I am."

– Bill Clinton, on missing the presidential music that accompanies the chief executive when he enters a room

## I WANT TO BE CORONATED

"People think that because I care so much about public issues, I should run for office myself. I don't want to run for office."

– Hillary Clinton, 1997

## FROM 40 MILES AWAY

"I've told a lot of people over the years that after the White House years I wanted to move to New York and have a chance to experience New York City and everything that goes with it."

– Hillary Clinton

## WE'RE STILL READY FOR OUR CLOSE-UPS, MR. DEMILLE!

"This is why they cannot retire from 'public service' when they leave the White House. This is why she is running for the Senate… She cannot live a life without power and admiration, or without the promise, the hope of power and admiration."

– Peggy Noonan

## "AND THIS WOMAN'S INITIALS SHOULD BE SOME COMBINATION OF 'RCH'"

"We will have a woman president by 2010."

– Hillary Clinton, 1992

## YOU'LL DO JUST FINE ON YOUR OWN, SENATOR

"I have said that I'm not running and I'm having a great time being pres— being a first-term senator…[Y]ou guys are going to get me into a lot of trouble."

– Hillary Clinton, to the National Press Club

## SOUNDS LIKE 16 YEARS OF HILL

"Eight years of Bill, eight years of Hill. That was the plan."

– Hillary Clinton, shortly after arriving in Washington, 1993

## NOT IN CHARGE, BUT STILL AT LARGE

"I sure do miss the work. There is just nothing like it."

– Bill Clinton, reflecting on his tenure and how he'd run the country if he were still at the helm, Hunter College, May 2002

## I'M JUST SAYIN'

"The 22nd Amendment should probably be modified to say two consecutive terms instead of two terms for a lifetime."

– Bill Clinton

## I'M STILL JUST SAYIN'

"There may come a time when we have elected a president at age 45 or 50 and then 20 years later the country comes up with the same sort of problems the president faced before, and the people would like to bring that man or woman back."

– Bill Clinton, speech at the John F. Kennedy Library and Museum, Boston, May 28, 2003

## YEAH, WE KNOW

"I may not have been the greatest president, but I've had the most fun eight years."

– Bill Clinton

## HE LIKED THE 'JOB'

"I like the job. That's what I'll miss the most… I'm not sure anybody ever liked this as much as I've liked it."

– Bill Clinton

"President Clinton will be moving out of the White House next week, and when he does he is expected to be the first president in history not to get his security deposit back."

– Jimmy Fallon, comedian, on "Saturday Night Live"

# 14

# The Martyrs

☆ ☆ ☆ ☆ ☆

### AND I FORESAKE YOU
"I'm oppressed like you. That's why you support me."

– Bill Clinton

### FIRST AMENDMENT (REVISED): FREEDOM FROM THE PRESS
"The press has a way of finding out everything about you if you become president."

– Bill Clinton, December 1993

### WOE IS SHE
"If someone has a female boss for the first time, maybe they can't take out their hostility on her, so they take it out on me."

– Hillary Clinton

### SO IS HE

"In the Bible it says they asked Jesus how many times you should forgive, and he said seventy times seven. Well, I want you to know that I'm keeping a chart."

– Hillary Clinton

### REPENTING…OR RESENTING?

"I've got to take this. I have to take this punishment. I don't know why God has chosen this for me, but He has… God is doing this, and He knows the reason."

– Hillary Clinton, to a friend during the Starr investigation

### HOW IS SHE SPELLING THAT?

"I've always been a praying person."

– Hillary Clinton, to a religious Boston audience, January 2005

## THE GIFT THAT JUST KEEPS ON GIVING

"The great story here for anybody willing to find it and write about it and explain it, is this vast right-wing conspiracy that has been conspiring against my husband since the day he announced for president."

– Hillary Clinton, on the "Today Show," January 27, 1998

## BREAKFAST OF CHAMPIONS

"That'll teach them to f--- with us."

– Hillary Clinton, to Linda Bloodworth-Thomason, at the White House after that morning's "Today Show" interview

## SO THEY REALLY WERE WITCHES

"I know about the Salem Witch Trials; I could sort of identify with those witches."

– Bill Clinton, speech at Salem State College, May 2001

## TINFOIL HATS, AISLE 3

"It has been clear to me for a number of years that there really is a vast, right-wing conspiracy. My only regret was using the word 'conspiracy' because there is absolutely nothing secret about it."

– Hillary Clinton, luncheon address to the American Constitution Society for Law and Policy, July 2003

## PLUS, BILL IS STILL IN HIS PJ'S

"What are you doing inviting these people into my home? These people are our enemies! They are trying to destroy us!"

– Hillary Clinton, to Rahm Emanuel, for inviting legislators to listen to a bipartisan panel that included James Baker, fall of 1993

## GOOD TO THE LAST EAVESDROP

"She received memos about the status of various press inquiries, she vetted senior campaign aides; and she listened to a secretly recorded audiotape of a phone conversation of Clinton critics plotting their next attack."

– Jeff Gerth and Don Van Natta, Jr., *Her Way*, regarding Hillary's spying activities during Bill Clinton's 1992 campaign, when it was illegal to intercept cell phone messages

## THE DOWNSIDE OF ANOTHER TERROR ATTACK

"It's a horrible prospect to ask yourself, 'What if? What if?' But if certain things happen between now and the election, particularly with respect to terrorism, that will automatically give the Republicans an advantage again, no matter how badly they have mishandled it, no matter how much more dangerous they have made the world."

– Hillary Clinton, to supporters in Concord, NH, August 23, 2007

## PAGING ROSIE AND BABS

"I believe in evil and I think that there are evil people in the world."

– Hillary Clinton

## A CENTER MADE OF RAINBOWS AND UNI-CORNS

"I long for the day when Republicans and Democrats will sit around and have these raucous, exciting arguments and actually love learning from one another, and when we create the common good out of a dynamic center."

– Bill Clinton, Georgetown University, October 18, 2006

## OR WE CAN WAIT

"F--- him, Bill. He's Reagan's G--damn Vice President."

– Hillary Clinton, to Bill, responding to George H.W. Bush's invitation to visit his home, mid 1980s

## MAJOR PAIN

"Only an idiot would buy the public persona of Bill Clinton... He is an incredibly profane individual. He is now and always has been an angry man who wants to inflict as much pain as possible on his enemies."

– Walter Erricson, retired reporter in Arkansas, *Capitol Hill Blue*, April 8, 1999

## SHE WANTS TO BE PRESIDENT OF WHICH PLANET?

"I mean, you've got a conservative and right-winged press presence with really nothing on the other end of the spectrum."

– Hillary Clinton, C-Span

# 15

# The Right-Wing Press

☆ ☆ ☆ ☆ ☆

## BACKWARD INDEED

"Hillary Rodham Clinton will define for women that magical spot where the important work of the world and love and children and an inner life all come together. Like Ginger Rogers, she will do everything her partner does, only backward and in high heels…"

– *TIME* correspondent Margaret Carlson, May 10, 1993

## THAT'S NOT HIS JAW!

"His sturdy jaw precedes him. He smiles from sea to shining sea. Is this president a candidate for Mt. Rushmore or what?"

– *L.A. Times* TV writer, reviewing Clinton's 1997 Inaugural Address

## PERFORM INDEED

"I'm endlessly fascinated by her... She's so smart. Virtually every time I've seen her perform, she has knocked my socks off."

– Lesley Stahl, about Hillary Clinton, December 1999

## TWO PEAS IN A POD

"Yes, I think he's an honest man...I do. Who among us has not lied about something? ...I know that you consider it sort of astonishing anybody would say so, but I think you can be an honest person and lie about any number of things."

– Dan Rather, May 15, 2001

# 16

# Their Sense of Irony

☆  ☆  ☆  ☆  ☆

## LONG LIVE THE QUEEN

"Some honestly believe they are motivated by the truth, they are motivated by a higher calling, they are motivated by, I guess, a direct line to the heavens."

– Hillary Clinton, ironically referring to the Republican majority in Congress, June 6, 2005

## AND SHE CAN COUNT HERS ON ONE HAND

"I think it will be very difficult, because the Republicans are a very disciplined, polished machine which intimidates opposition. Still, there comes a time when the truth has to count for something."

– Hillary Clinton, response to whether G.W. Bush could be beaten in 2004, August 2003

## WISHFUL THINKING

"Desperate Housewives."

– Bill Clinton, relating his favorite TV show, 2003

## AS DOES THE ROAD FROM HOPE

"The road to tyranny, we must remember, begins with the destruction of the truth."

– Bill Clinton, speech at the University of Connecticut, October 15, 1997

## IS THAT A COMPLIMENT?

"But you know, you have got to hand it to them. These Republicans are ruthless and they are relentless."

– Hillary Clinton

"She is one of the most ruthless people we have ever seen in politics."

– Dick Morris, former Clinton adviser

## AT LEAST HE'D *ASK* THIS JUANITA

"You know, if I were a single man, I might ask that mummy out. That's a good-looking mummy!"

– Bill Clinton, about a recently discovered Inca mummy named Juanita, June 17, 1996

## BEFORE OR AFTER YOU AND BILL MOVED TO THE NEIGHBORHOOD?

"We've had a steep increase in the number of reported rapes here in New York City."

– Hillary Clinton, to *The New York Times*, April 2002

## ANITA HILL—OR PAULA JONES?

"She has transformed consciousness and changed history with her courageous testimony."

– Hillary Clinton, at an award ceremony for Anita Hill by the American Bar Association, 1992

## WE SHOULD THINK SO!

"I have a pretty good antenna for people who are chauvinistic or sexist or patronizing toward women."

– Hillary Clinton

## SHE FEELS YOUR PAIN (ALL THE WAY FROM CHAPPAQUA)

"The leadership in this city refuses to reach out, to work with a community that is in pain, to even acknowledge there is a problem."

– Hillary Clinton, referring to the Giuliani administration while campaigning for Senate

## REACHING OUT
"Well, good."

– Hillary Clinton, in response to a man telling her he's homeless as she campaigned for Bill, 1992

## IS THAT WHY THEY'RE BEST FRIENDS?
"Every time [George H. W.] Bush talks about trust it makes chills run up and down my spine. The way he has trampled on the truth is a travesty of the American political system."

– Bill Clinton, October 28, 1992

## WHICH REPUBLIC?
"Mine will be the most ethical administration in the history of the Republic."

– Bill Clinton, blasting the standards of behavior of the first Bush administration, November 1992

## SO THAT I MIGHT BECOME ACQUAINTED WITH IT
"I ask that all Americans demonstrate in their personal and public lives...the high ethical standards that are essential to good character and to the continued success of our nation."

– President Bill Clinton, October 17, 1997

## AND HE MEANS *ALL* KINDS OF GIVING

"I've done my best in this book to demonstrate what I've seen firsthand through my foundation's work in Africa and around the world: that all kinds of giving can make a profoundly positive difference."

– Bill Clinton, August 2007, on his new book *Giving: How Each of Us Can Change the World*, about citizen activism and public service, by the man who took the "L" out of public service

## BRING YOUR CIGARS!

"Oh my goodness, I feel like we are going to get into the White House again and we are going to walk around and say where do we start to clean up this mess? ...Bring your vacuum cleaners, bring your brushes, bring your brooms, bring your mops."

– Hillary Clinton, to ABC News, November 5, 2007

"Everywhere they go, they leave a trail of disappointed, disillusioned friends and staff members to clean up after them. The Clintons' only loyalty is to their own ambitions...[Bill and Hillary Clinton are] grifters. Grifters was a term used in the Great Depression to describe fast-talking con-artists who roamed the countryside, profiting at the expense of the poor and the uneducated, always one step ahead of the law, moving on before they were held accountable for their schemes and half-truths."

– Jimmy Carter's former Chief of Staff, *The Wall Street Journal*, February 20, 2001

## NOT MY GOLDFISH, HE HAS A TINFOIL HAT

"Before this is over, they'll attack me, they'll attack you, they'll attack your cat, they'll attack your goldfish."

– Hillary Clinton, explaining politics to Chelsea, upon her father's entrance into the presidential race, 1992

## BULLSEYE DID NOT HAVE A TINFOIL HAT

"That's too bad. Bullseye was his name, wasn't it? You're just not getting the message, are you?"

– A Hillary henchman, to Kathleen Willey, soon after three of her tires had been nail-gunned and her 13-year-old cat Bullseye went missing, January 8, 1998

## IT'S ACTUALLY PRONOUNCED 'SHAME US'

"Former President Clinton's new dog is named 'Seamus,' ABC News has learned."

– ABC News, referring to a third Clinton dog despite two previous ones being run over while running loose, June 5, 2002

**17**

# Their Love of Animals

☆　☆　☆　☆　☆

"A righteous man regardeth the life of his beast: but the tender mercies of the wicked are cruel."

– Proverbs (12:10)

### WHILE ATTEMPTING TO JOIN HIS MASTER IN LOOKING FOR TAIL

"Former President Bill Clinton's dog Buddy was killed Wednesday by a passing car outside the family's Westchester County, New York home."

– CNN.com, January 2, 2002

### SPEEDBUMP BUDDY

"Everybody's sad. But it's funny. A lot of people have been calling me asking shouldn't they have somebody watching the dog? I said, well, yeah."

– Clinton neighbor, referring to Buddy not being kenneled or supervised while the Clintons were on vacation in Acapulco

## AND THEN THERE WERE NONE

"We understand that Buddy is the second Clinton family dog to be killed in traffic. Please let him be the last."

– Ingrid Newkirk, president of PETA

## BULLSEYE!

"Twelve years ago the family's first dog, Zeke…was also killed by a car while running loose… During the 1992 presidential campaign, Hillary Clinton explained to an acquaintance that Zeke was killed 'after years of near misses.'"

– Newsmax, January 4, 2002

## LIKE MASTER, LIKE BEAST

"The dog reportedly escaped the mansion grounds regularly and prowled the Quapaw Quarter, where he sired a few puppies. After complaints from neighbors, the Clintons decided to neuter Zeke."

– *Arkansas Democrat-Gazette*, 1998

## THEY DO TRAVEL IN PACKS

"Buddy, the dog, came along to keep Bill company. He was the only member of our family who was still willing to."

– Hillary Clinton, referring to their Martha's Vineyard retreat after Bill's grand jury testimony, *Living History*

## ZEKE...OR BILL?

"Local sources say Hillary Clinton didn't like it in the house."

– WorldNetDaily.com, March 20, 2002

"I wouldn't want any un-neutered Clintons in my house."

– Linda Chavez, former Labor Secretary nominee, who offered to adopt the Clintons' cat Socks and asked if he was fixed

## FROM THE INBREDS WHO WOULD HAVE ONLY PUREBREDS...

"[Hillary] Clinton wrote a crowd-pleasing book *Dear Socks, Dear Buddy: Kids' Letters to the First Pets*, in which she claimed that only with the arrival of Socks and his 'toy mouse' did the White House 'become a home.' Being Clinton, she also lectured readers that pets are an 'adoption instead of an acquisition' and warned them to look out for their safety."

– *Sunday Times of London*, October 21, 2007

## BITES TO BE BUDDY; SUCKS TO BE SOX

"Turns out the former first couple didn't allow Buddy or first cat Socks in the White House residence, according to the Army vet."

– WorldNetDaily.com, interview with the White House veterinarian after Buddy's death, March 20, 2002

## STICK-STUCK

"Scene to Remember: In 1998, Clinton throws stick to Buddy on his way to his car. Buddy runs long to fetch stick. Master steps into limousine and glides away. Buddy brings back stick and finds no one to give it to. Drops stick on lawn. Wanders away."

– EtherZone.com, January 11, 2002

## HAS ANYONE SEEN SEAMUS LATELY?

"Don't forget, even though I won't be the president, I'll always be with you till the last dog dies."

– Bill Clinton, in New Hampshire, January 2001

**18**

# Others on Bill

☆ ☆ ☆ ☆ ☆

## DOESN'T SEEM THAT TORN

"Last time I saw him he was swinging on the chandelier in the Oval Office with a brassiere around his head, Viagra in one hand and a Bible in the other, and he was torn between good and evil."

– Congressman James Traficant, Jr. (D-Oh.), in *The Washington Post*, September 11, 1998

## OH IT'S PRETTY BASIC, ALL RIGHT

"President Clinton is working to project a more decisive image, because—much to his surprise and contrary to his character—there seems to be a perception that he has no basic value system."

– Helen Thomas, former White House correspondent for United Press International

## CHATTY CATHY

"We give him Hemingway. He'll turn it into Faulkner."

– Michael Waldman, White House speechwriter, 1993–99, on Clinton's tendency to run on during speeches

## HOW TO STAY A FEMINIST IN THE AGE OF BILL CLINTON

"I mean, all of us knew he was a snake when we voted for him."

– President of the National Organization of Women, 1998

## WANNA BET?

"Clinton is far more psychologically disturbed than the public ever imagined."

– *Newsweek*, April 7, 1999

## YOU'D HAVE TO GET WHACKED

"[D]efending President Clinton is like being in the Mafia—you just can't get out of the thing. I'm like Michael Corleone. How do I get out of this business?"

– James Carville, January 2002

## GETTING OUT THE HARD WAY

"I just got sick and tired of lying for the fella."

– Jim McDougal, deceased former Clinton business partner

## HE CAN'T THRIVE AT 55

"If [his polls] reach 60 percent, then he can start dating again."

– Fritz Hollings, former Democratic senator from South Carolina, 1998

## THE SUM OF TALL BEERS

"One of the most charismatic men I've ever met, but I was less impressed with his substance."

– Tom Clancy, author, interview, 1997

"Clinton is saying he's going to model his after-presidential life after Jimmy Carter. He'll be doing a lot of hammering and a lot of nailing, but he ain't building houses."

– David Letterman, comedian

"[If] somebody were to make a life-sized replica of Bill Clinton entirely out of margarine, WD-40, and banana peels, it would still be less slippery than the original."

– Dennis Miller, comedian

"Bill Clinton treats the truth like your mom treats the good china. There's never an occasion special enough to actually use it, although you can take it out and look at once in a while."

– Dennis Miller, comedian

# 19

# Women on Bill

☆ ☆ ☆ ☆ ☆

### ACTORS: AS INTELLIGENT ASLEEP AS AWAKE
"The only two sexual dreams I've ever had were about [Bill Clinton]."

– Rose McGowan, actress

### NOTHING COMPARES, NOTHING COMPARES ...TO BILL
"Does impeachment mean they're going to turn him into a peach? If so, can I eat him?"

– Sinead O'Connor, singer

### SWEET NOTHINGS
"Can anyone remember a single meaningful phrase Clinton ever uttered?"

– Ann Coulter

## STRANGE DAYS

"It was very strange. He did say, 'I am sorry,' but he then went into this discussion about the fact that he had been so angry and none of us understood about what. That is what got confusing."

– Madeleine Albright, regarding the 1998 meeting in which Bill Clinton apologized to his Cabinet for the Lewinsky affair, September 2003

# 20

# Others on Hillary

☆ ☆ ☆ ☆ ☆

## YOU'VE COME A LONG WAY...FROM YOUR-SELF

"I am not saying she has learnt to be herself. I think after a year on the trail she has learnt how not to be herself, how to comfortably adopt a skin and play a part."

– Peggy Noonan, October 21, 2007

## BILL AND HILL AS SOULMATES

"She has this unbelievable ability to be a liar. She is soulless."

– Former Hillary Senate campaign worker

## BULL-DOZER

"I mean, she's a scary woman. She'll go after what she believes in and I doubt that anyone could stand up to her."

– Susan McDougal, who endorsed Hillary for both the Senate and the presidency

## FROSTY WINDOW TO THE SOUL

"The kid [Chelsea] ran right to [Bill Clinton] and never once looked at her mother... I could see that she had a warm relationship with him, but was almost afraid of her mother. Hillary is ice-cold. You can see it in her eyes."

– Richard Nixon, on his unlikely afternoon visit with the Clintons, March 1993

# 21

# Clintelligence

☆ ☆ ☆ ☆ ☆

**AND PASS THE DOOBIE**

"When Members of Congress and others come in and get all heated up and angry over some issue, I often call a time out, and I say, 'Wait a minute. See that rock? It came off the Moon. It's 3.6 billion years old. We're all just passing through. Chill out.'"

– Bill Clinton, March 20, 2000

**IF HE DOES SAY SO HIMSELF**

"There will come a time when we can look back and say, 'Well, who should have done what when.' And it ought to be done. But now is not the time."

– Bill Clinton, objecting to a congressional investigation into intelligence failures leading to the September 11th attacks, on "Good Morning America," October 2001

## ICH BIN EIN TERRORISTER

"First of all, terror…has a very long history. Here in the United States, we were founded as a nation that practiced slavery and slaves were, quite frequently, killed even though they were innocent. This country once looked the other way when significant numbers of Native Americans were dispossessed and killed to get their land or their mineral rights… And even today we still have the occasional hate crime rooted in race, religion, or sexual orientation. So terror has a long history."

– Bill Clinton, speech at Georgetown University, two months after September 11, 2001

## MY SHORT MEMORY

"My Life."

– Title of Bill Clinton's thousand-page memoir

## IT GETS EASIER WITH PRACTICE

"I'm trying to be honest with you and it hurts me."

– Bill Clinton, grand jury testimony, August 17, 1998

## STAY TUNED

"Before I came to the White House, I dealt with people in a very direct way. If something was on my mind, I said it."

– Hillary Clinton

## TO ILLEGAL ALIENS

"It makes a lot of sense."

– Hillary Clinton, in New Hampshire, defending New York Governor Eliot Spitzer's plan to allow illegal immigrants to obtain drivers' licenses, October 2007

## ESPECIALLY SINCE OUR VOTING BASE IS DEAD PEOPLE, ILLEGAL IMMIGRANTS, FELONS, AND CANINES

"I just want to add, I did not say that it should be done, but I certainly recognize why Governor Spitzer is trying to do it."

– Hillary Clinton, on the same issue after fellow Democratic candidate Chris Dodd attacked the idea

### WHICH IS A REDUCTION OF ABOUT 50%

"Unless I missed something, Senator Clinton said two different things in the course of about two minutes."

– John Edwards, Democratic debate, Philadelphia, October 30, 2007

## ASK SENATOR BYRD

"Just try to imagine what it would be like to be three hundred million years old."

– Bill Clinton, referring to the New River, America's oldest river, Ashe County, North Carolina, July 30, 1998

## EXCEPT FOR ROSS PEROT, PHIL GRAMM, AND GEORGE H. W. BUSH

"I'm sure I spent more time in Texas than anybody else who had run for president recently."

– Bill Clinton, Longview, Texas, September 27, 1996

## CALLED DEPRAVITY-PALOOZA

"Last year, the vice president launched a new effort to help make communities more liberal."

– Bill Clinton, during his 2000 State of the Union speech, intending to say "more livable" and repeating the slip-up a few sentences later

## HYDROPONICS, DUDE!

"I am the only president who knew something about agriculture when I got there."

– Bill Clinton, to a group of Iowa farmers, forgetting the farmers Carter, Truman, Jefferson, and Washington, 1995

## AS WINE

"I have probably consumed more raisins than any president who ever held this office."

– Bill Clinton, to a group of school children in Selma, CA, the "raisin capital of the world"

## SHOCK AND AW-SHUCKS

"Clinton wants us to pay for the education of children in other countries because 'it's a lot cheaper than going to war.' This kind of talk is considered Deep Stuff by shallow people."

– Thomas Sowell, syndicated columnist, November 16, 2001

## EXCEPT YOU AVOIDED PRISON

"I'm making my annual trek to Africa to see the work of my AIDS and development project, and to celebrate with Nelson Mandela his birthday. He's 89. Don't know how many more he'll have. And when I think that I might be 99.9 percent the same as him, I can't even fathom it."

– Bill Clinton, Harvard College Class Day, June 6, 2007

## YOU FIRST

"Get tested, tested, tested."

– Bill Clinton, advice concerning AIDS

## SOMEONE PLEASE GET THE EXTERMINA-TOR

"One of my husband's favorite old Southern sayings…is that if you find a turtle on a fence post, it didn't get there by accident. And I just look at the landscape around here and I see lots of big old turtles sitting on lots of fenceposts. I think we need to find out how those old turtles got on those fenceposts."

– Hillary Clinton, a day after she blamed the sex allegations against her husband on a "vast right-wing conspiracy," January 28, 1998

## THE SAP GETS THICKER

"If this isn't good for my heart, I don't know what is."

– Bill Clinton, reacting to applause while stumping for John Kerry after Clinton's quadruple bypass surgery, Love Park, Philadelphia, October 25, 2004

## WHITE HOUSE...OR WAFFLE HOUSE?

"Well, that's not my decision to make."

– Hillary Clinton, response to Tim Russert's question at a Democratic debate, on whether she would release communications between herself and the president when she was first lady, October 30, 2007

# 22

# And to All the Little People Out There

☆　☆　☆　☆　☆

## THE HYPOCRITIC OATH

"Or maybe somebody else says: 'You know, I'm going to start thanking the woman who cleans the restroom in the building that I work in.' You know, maybe that sounds kind of stupid, but on the other hand I want to start seeing her as a human being."

– Hillary Clinton, speech a few weeks before she fired everyone in the White House travel office, 1993

## PRESCHOOLERS: NOT PART OF THE GREATER GOOD

"I want to get this s--- over with and get these damn people out of here."

– Hillary Clinton, referring to preschoolers posing for a photograph on the lawn of the Governor's Mansion, Arkansas

## THEN AGAIN...

"The story is true, but I don't really want to comment any further. We were expecting Mr. Clinton, but he never arrived and he didn't even cancel his reservation."

–Restaurant owner in Rome, who took down a reservation for Clinton's party of 18 and spent a thousand dollars ordering in extra food and wine after the security team checked the place out and confirmed, May 2005

## BILL AND THE BILL

"They bloody well did not pay the bill... I wouldn't quite say he did a runner. I just don't think it occurred to him to pay."

– Owner of a Notting Hill pub, to *The Guardian* newspaper, when President Clinton had a $36 lunch and left without paying the bill, after a morning of tea with Queen Elizabeth at Buckingham Palace, December 2000

## DID YOU HEAR THE ONE ABOUT THE SINGLE MOM WHO MAKES LESS THAN MINIMUM WAGE AND SERVED HILLARY BREAKFAST ON THE HOUSE...

"No comment."

– Hillary campaign staffer, when asked what the first lady's share was in the $100 savings bond that the staff pitched in to send to a waitress whom Hillary was found to have not tipped at the Village House in Albion, NY, February 2000

## DO AS I SAY...

"In the central highlands in Africa where I work, people meet each other walking on the trails, and one person says hello, how are you, good morning, the answer is not I'm fine, how are you. The answer translated into English is this: 'I see you.' Think of that. I see you. How many people do all of us pass every day that we never see?"

– Bill Clinton, Harvard College Class Day, June 6, 2007

## ...NOT AS I DO

"The least pleasant of all was Bill Clinton... Clinton was very demanding, cold and always occupied. He was unaware of me completely."

– Georges de Paris, official tailor to the White House

## THAT'S OKAY, SOCIALIZED MEDICINE, RE-MEMBER?

"The van went by me and we ordered them to stop and it continued going and we continued to yell to stop. At that point I banged as hard as I could on the side of the van to let the driver know he had to stop."

– Police officer, at Westchester County Airport, who injured his arm when Hillary Clinton's van tried to blow past a mandatory checkpoint during a heightened state of alert after the 9/11 attacks, October 14, 2001

## BUT IT'S CLINTON, SO WHO'S COUNTING?

"Characteristically more than 90 minutes late, Clinton whipped up the partisan crowd with the message that Democrats have to keep a 'check' on Republicans in power in Washington and Little Rock... People began arriving for the scheduled 4:30 rally at 2 p.m. but, by the time Clinton arrived after 6 p.m., only a third of the 1,147-seat auditorium was filled."

– *The Commercial Appeal*, West Memphis, Arkansas, August 2002

# 23

# Did I Stutter...or Slur?

☆  ☆  ☆  ☆  ☆

**TICK, TICK, TICK**

"I have in the past certainly, you know maybe, called somebody a name. But I have never used an ethnic, racial, anti-Semitic, bigoted, discriminatory, prejudiced, accusation against anybody."

– Hillary Clinton, from CNN.com, July 16, 2000

**KABOOM**

"She's a short, Irish b----."

– Hillary Clinton, on columnist Maureen Dowd

**SO THE CHILDREN DON'T END UP LIKE ME**

"Within and beyond their homes, adults must speak against racial, ethnic, religious, or gender slurs."

– Hillary Clinton, *It Takes a Village*

## OY-PAY

"That's all you people think about is money."

– Hillary Clinton, to Dick Morris, Jewish campaign adviser, when he asked for a raise

## BUT BEING MULTICULTURALISTS

"That little Greek motherf----!"

– Bill Clinton, after the Dukakis team made fun of his long, self-centered speech at the 1988 Democratic National Convention

## I'M HERE ALL WEEK, TRY THE VEAL

"I love this quote. It's from Mahatma Gandhi. He had a gas station down in St. Louis for a couple of years. Mr. Gandhi, you still own that gas station? A lot of wisdom comes out of that gas station."

– Hillary Clinton, fundraiser for Nancy Farmer, St. Louis, January 3, 2004

## ISN'T SHE PRO-CHOICE?

"Every time we let a religious or racial slur go unchallenged or an indignity go unanswered, we are making a choice to be indifferent…a choice, I believe, to ignore history at our children's peril."

– Hillary Clinton, Millennium Dinner at the White House, April 12, 1999

# 24

# With Peacemakers Like These...

☆　☆　☆　☆　☆

## THE BUBBA GUIDE TO FOREIGN POLICY

"Lee, I've been traveling around our country for a year and no one cares about foreign policy other than about six journalists."

– President Bill Clinton, interrupting Rep. Hamilton of the Foreign Affairs Committee, when the latter gave a rundown of the foreign policy hot potatoes he'd have to deal with, 1992

## THAT'S WHAT SHE SAID

"God, it's hard. It's the hardest thing I've ever seen."

– Bill Clinton, to the *New York Daily News* during the Camp David Summit, July 2000

"It's really quite tragic."

– Bill Clinton, concerning the Palestinian-Israeli conflict, Hay-on-Wye Festival, Wales, May 2001

## WHAT THE TWO OF THEM DID TOGETHER IS NOBODY'S BUSINESS

"President Clinton met with [Arafat] more often than with any other international leader (24 times in eight years)."

– Accuracy in Media, November 12, 2004

## HE BEEN ROBBED!

"Just last month, Mr. Clinton, in an interview with Newsweek, blamed Arafat for destroying his 'legacy.'"

– JewishWorldReview.com, July 13, 2001

## HE WANTS TO BE ROBBED AGAIN

"If [Hamas] made the same assurances that Arafat did…I would support dealing with them."

– Bill Clinton, to BBC, on whether he would negotiate with Hamas, April Fool's Day 2006

## FOREIGN POLICY PRESS BRIEFING DURING THE CLINTON ERA

"I think we took you up through the two bilaterals that happened late in the afternoon. After that, the president, the two leaders, and their delegations—somewhere around 40 people—had dinner together in the Laurel Cabin. They dined on tenderloin of beef with sun-dried tomatoes, fillet of salmon with Thai curry sauce, roast baby Yukon potatoes, steamed green beans with almonds, a mixed garden salad, fresh fruit, and assorted desserts."

– White House Spokesman Joe Lockhart, near Camp David, Maryland, summer of 2000

## WHAT? I'M NOT IN THE STATE DEPARTMENT?

"I think it will be in the long-term interests of the Middle East for Palestine to be a state."

– Hillary Clinton, May 6, 1998

## A FEW YEARS PREMATURE

"These remarks are her own personal view. The administration's position on this matter has not changed."

– The U.S. consulate in Jerusalem, the next day, distancing the administration from the first lady's statement

## THEY CAN ALL SHARE THE ONE GAS MASK

"Expressing her solidarity with Israel, Senator Hillary Rodham Clinton (D-NY) has donated $1,200 to purchase protective gear for Israeli teachers and medics in the West Bank and Gaza Strip."

– *The Jerusalem Post*, April 4, 2001

### IN A DR. KEVORKIAN SORT OF WAY

"[President Clinton] is the best friend Israel ever had in the White House."

– Al Gore, to *The Jewish Press*, November 2000

### NOT BECAUSE YOU WERE LATE FOR "FRIENDS"?

"I can tell you that the decisions we made, we made because we thought they were in the interests of the American people."

– Bill Clinton, on why he went against the Pentagon and signed waivers to sell Loral missile guidance technology to Red China

### FOR-ME POLICY

"His foreign policy was basically to get re-elected…that took precedence over everything else."

– Casper Weinberger, about Bill Clinton, November 2001

### WHO BOMBED WHAT? NOT NOW—I'M BUSY

"President Clinton did not visit the World Trade Center in 1993… Four days after the attack, Mr. Clinton was across the Hudson River in New Brunswick, NJ, discussing job-training programs. There, he urged the public not to 'overreact' to the World Trade Center bombing. But he didn't cross the river and see the damage for himself."

– Richard Miniter, *Losing bin Laden: How Bill Clinton's Failures Unleashed Global Terror*

## THE PARROT CHIMES IN

"It's been said, and I think it's accurate, that my husband was obsessed by terrorism in general and al-Qaeda in particular."

– Hillary Clinton, April 16, 2004

## HE SHOULD HAVE WORN A THONG

"By Clinton's own account, Monica Lewinsky was able to visit him privately more than a dozen times in the Oval Office. But according to a *USA Today* investigative report, the head of the CIA could not get a single private meeting with the president, despite the Trade Center bombing of February 26, 1993 or the killing of 18 American soldiers in Mogadishu on October 3rd of the same year."

– FrontPageMag.com, March 24, 2004

## CLUCKING IDIOT

"[Clinton's] approach to fighting terrorism at a 1996 antiterrorism summit in Egypt—which State Department cables reveal was subordinated to Clinton's personal back-door effort to get Russia to buy more frozen Arkansas chicken—earned the label 'chicken diplomacy.'"

– *Insight* magazine, November 13, 2000

## CAN'T OR WON'T?

"I can't answer that question."

– Former Secretary of State Madeleine Albright, response to Tim Russert asking why Bill Clinton turned down a deal with Sudan to take Osama bin Laden into custody

## FORGET THE TERRORISTS, LET'S FIGHT CUMULONIMBUS

"First, I worry about climate change. It's the only thing that I believe has the power to fundamentally end the march of civilization as we know it."

– Bill Clinton, World Economic Forum, Davos, January, 2006

## I DON'T WANT TO POINT ANY FINGERS, BUT...

"We have succeeded to a remarkable degree, since September 11th, to not let this thing become a partisan issue... All I know is that, at least in my time, more of these things were prevented than occurred..."

– Bill Clinton, to Rita Cosby, on Fox News Channel

## ESPECIALLY WHEN CRUISE MISSILES WILL DISTRACT FROM MY INFIDELITY

"We always believed that responding faster was better."

– Bill Clinton, on the phone with B.E.T. during a televised Katrina fundraiser, contrasting his administration with Bush's amid accusations of a slow federal response, 2005

## I CAN CRY ON CUE

"I said to Clinton, 'Do you wish you were president now?' and he said, 'I feel I would be better trained for it, more prepared.'"

– Paul McCartney's then fiancé Heather Mills, to *The New York Post*, October 2001

## I WOULD STAND INSTEAD

"I promised myself when I left the presidency that I would not spend one day sitting and moping and wishing I was still president."

– Bill Clinton, to *Fortune* magazine

## USUALLY OF MY OWN MAKING

"There have been many times since then [leaving office] that I wish I had been able to help the American people and the world with problems that come across the president's desk."

– Bill Clinton, to Peter Jennings, November 18, 2004

### WRITTEN ON HAPPY MEAL WRAPPERS

"We left a comprehensive anti-terror strategy [for the incoming Bush team]."

– Bill Clinton, "Fox News Sunday," September 24, 2006

### DID YOU CHECK UNDER THE PINBALL MACHINE?

"We were not left a comprehensive strategy to fight al Qaeda."

– Secretary of State Condoleezza Rice, September 25, 2006

### NORTH KOREA POPS BACK INTO THE HEADLINES, SO DOES BILL

"We actually drew up plans to attack North Korea and to destroy their reactors and we told them we would attack unless they ended their nuclear program."

– Bill Clinton, to a security forum in Rotterdam, Netherlands, when North Korea announced plans to restart building its nuclear reactor, December 2002

### CLICK YOUR HEELS THREE TIMES

"We did a lot of good. We did. We did a lot of good."

– Bill Clinton, in an unprecedented speech by an outgoing president saluting himself upon the new president's inauguration, January 20, 2001

## FEELING A BIT KIM JONG IL TO MY STOMACH

"We had a tough time with [North Korea], but we got them to end that program and they kept it ended until apparently today they started again. They would have a hundred weapons if we hadn't done that."

– Bill Clinton, on "Larry King Live," February 6, 2003

"Not only did he know [that North Korea has restarted its nuclear program], but while he knew, he was pressing Congress to give [the Koreans] food and fuel to honor his '94 agreement [with Pyongyang]."

– Dick Morris, February 10, 2003

## AT LEAST BILL CLINTON DIDN'T ALIENATE EUROPE...HE BOMBED IT

"We act to prevent a wider war... Let a fire burn here in this area and the flames will spread."

– Bill Clinton, statement to the American people explaining why NATO is bombing Christian Serbs on behalf of Muslim Albanians in Kosovo, who were being "ethnically cleansed," March 25, 1999

## OOPS

"We did not find one—not one—mass grave… There never was a genocide in Kosovo. It was dishonest and wrong for western leaders to adopt the term in the beginning to give moral authority to the operation."

– Spanish forensic investigator, in interviews with the *Sunday Times of London* and Spain's *El Pais* newspaper

## IF YOU WANT ETHNIC CLEANSING DONE RIGHT, YOU HAVE TO DO IT YOURSELF

"Perversely, the large-scale population displacement NATO was ostensibly acting to prevent began only after the bombs started falling."

– Christopher Deliso, *The Coming Balkan Caliphate*

## ONLY ONE MAN COULD HELP BILL CLINTON IN HIS HOUR OF NEEDING A WAR

"Osama bin Laden's al-Qaeda terrorist network has been active in the Balkans for years, most recently helping Kosovo rebels battle for independence from Serbia with the financial and military backing of the United States and NATO."

– *The Wall Street Journal-Europe*, November 1, 2001

## ANTI-WAR MOVEMENT...MIA

"It wasn't very hip."

– Janeane Garofalo, response to why there wasn't a peace movement protesting Bill Clinton's wars, on "Fox News Sunday," February 23, 2003

# 25

# From Here to Clinternity

☆ ☆ ☆ ☆ ☆

## PLEASE DON'T ADD TO YOUR EXTENSIVE REPERTOIRE; THE CIGAR WAS INNOVATIVE ENOUGH

"I'm still young enough to learn how to do new and different things… I just need a little time to get my bearings, and I just hope I'm not too old to change."

– Bill Clinton, in *Rolling Stone*, October 2000

## I WASN'T A PRESIDENT, BUT I COULD PLAY ONE ON TV

"If President Reagan could be an actor and become president, maybe I could become an actor. I've got a good pension. I can work for cheap."

– Bill Clinton, at a Hollywood fundraiser

## PICKS HIS WORDS LIKE HE PICKS HIS WOMEN: QUANTITY OVER QUALITY

"Public records housed [at the Clinton Library] will chronicle history's wordiest president, in an abundance unmatched at other presidential repositories. They include a mountain of paper, some 76.8 million pages, plus 40 million e-mails…"

– *The Washington Times*, July 19, 2002

## WE FEEL A YAWN COMING ON

"I'll never get tired of living."

– Bill Clinton, while recovering from his heart operation, September 2004

## OTHERWISE WE CAN EXPECT THE 1000-PAGE SEQUEL; *MY DEATH*

"Even when he dies, we better make sure the coffin's nailed shut."

– Douglas Brinkley, historian